W9-BCN-976

DOGS

LABRADOR RETRIEVERS

STUART A. KALLEN

ABDO & Daughters

6839955

Published by Abdo & Daughters, 4940 Viking Drive, Suite 622, Edina, Minnesota 55435.

Library bound edition distributed by Rockbottom Books, Pentagon Tower, P.O. Box 36036, Minneapolis, Minnesota 55435.

Copyright © 1996 by Abdo Consulting Group, Inc., Pentagon Tower, P.O. Box 36036, Minneapolis, Minnesota 55435 USA. International copyrights reserved in all countries. No part of this book may be reproduced in any form without written permission from the publisher.

Printed in the United States.

Cover Photo credit: Peter Arnold, Inc.

Interior Photo credits: Peter Arnold, Inc.

Edited by Rosemary Wallner

Library of Congress Cataloging-in-Publication Data

Kallen, Stuart A., 1955
        Labrador retriever / Stuart A. Kallen.
        p. cm. — (Dogs)
Includes bibliographical references (p.24) and index.
ISBN 1-56239-453-3
1. Labrador retriever—Juvenile literature. [1. Labrador retriever. 2. Dogs.] I. Title.
II. Series: Kallen, Stuart A., 1955- Dogs.
SF429.L3K34   1995
636.7'52—dc20   95-1510
                                                              CIP
                                                              AC

ABOUT THE AUTHOR

Stuart Kallen has written over 80 children's books, including many environmental science books.

Contents

DOGS AND WOLVES: CLOSE COUSINS

Dogs have been living with humans for more than 12,000 years. Today, hundreds of millions of dogs live in the world. Over 400 **breeds** exist.

All dogs are related to the wolf. Some dogs—like tiny poodles or Great Danes—may look nothing like the wolf. But under their skin, all dogs share the same **instincts** and **traits** as the wolf.

The dog family is called **Canidae**, from the Latin word meaning "dog." The canid family has 37 **species**, including foxes, jackals, wild dogs, and wolves.

All dogs are related to the wolf. Dogs may not look like wolves, but they share the same instincts.

LABRADOR RETRIEVERS

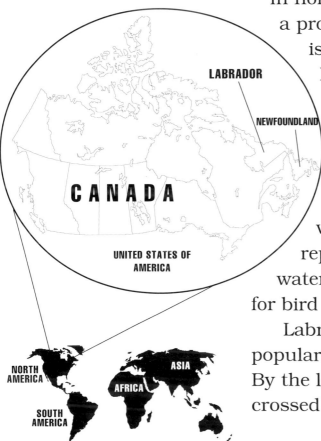

In northeastern Canada, there is a province called Labrador. An island off the coast of Labrador is called Newfoundland. This is the home of the Labrador **retriever**. No one knows how Labs first came to live there. But in 1822, a visitor to the island reported seeing a "small water dog...trained as a retriever for bird hunting."

Labradors quickly became popular for their hunting abilities. By the late 1800s, Labs were crossed with other sporting dogs

Labradors have become popular for their hunting abilities.

such as the flat-coat **retriever** and the tweed water spaniel. Today, hunters prize the Labrador for its quick running and swimming, and its fine sense of smell.

WHAT THEY'RE LIKE

Throughout the world, people love and respect Labrador **retrievers**. They use them as war dogs, police dogs, and guides for the blind. These dogs are mighty swimmers. They will jump into freezing water to save someone.

In World War II, Labs carried packs with important messages for the armed services. They sniffed out booby traps and mines. Soldiers even taught them to wear parachutes and jump from airplanes!

Labs are helpful in disasters. They can obey hand signals and will run through smoke and broken glass to find people who are hurt.

Labradors are even-tempered, smart, strong, and healthy.

Labradors are even-tempered, happy dogs that are healthy and strong.

COAT AND COLOR

Labrador **retrievers** are black, yellow, or chocolate colored. Sometimes black Labs have a small patch of white on their chest. Yellow Labs can be any color from ivory white to copper red. Chocolate colored Labs range from dark brown to a light tan.

A Lab's tail is called an "otter tail." It is covered with the same kind of thick, dense fur that's on the rest of the Lab. Labs carry their tail high, not curved over the back.

Labrador retrievers have two **coats** of fur. The outer coat is thick and dense. The hairs are straight and stiff. The second coat is called the undercoat. This coat is waterproof. The undercoat keeps the Lab warm in cold temperatures and in cold water.

A chocolate-colored Labrador's coat is shiny brown.

SIZE

Labs are strong, short, and solid. Male Labs stand 22 to 25 inches (56 to 64 cm) at the shoulders. Male Labs weigh 60 to 70 pounds (27 to 32 kg). Female Labs are about an inch (2.5 cm) shorter and 5 pounds (2 kg) lighter.

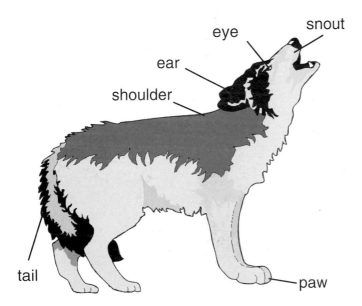

A Lab's head is well-shaped. A healthy Lab has no fleshiness in its cheeks and no loose skin under its jaws. The medium-sized ears hang close to the head.

All dogs share the same features with their common ancestor, the wolf.

A healthy Lab has no fleshiness in its cheeks and no loose skin under its jaws.

CARE

Dogs need the same things that humans need: a warm bed, food, water, and lots of love.

A dog lives for about 17 years. Labs enjoy human contact and like to **retrieve** sticks or catch Frisbees.

You'll need to brush your Lab once every week to remove dead and matted hair. Sometimes, the dog will need a bath and its nails clipped.

All dogs need shots every year. These shots stop diseases such as **distemper** and **hepatitis**.

Young puppies must be watched closely. They could get in trouble with cars, other dogs, or wild animals.

Labs are lovable dogs and thrive on contact.

FEEDING

Strong, stocky dogs like Labs need more food than an average smaller dog. Like all dogs, Labs enjoy meat. But Labs need a well-balanced diet. Most dog foods—dry or canned—will provide Labs with the proper **nutrition**.

Dogs should not be fed table scraps during mealtimes. This will make the dog a beggar.

Large beef bones help keep a dog's teeth healthy. Never give a dog small bones or chicken bones. These bones splinter and could choke the animal.

Like any animal, Labs need a lot of fresh water. Water should be kept next to their food bowl and changed daily.

Labradors need more food than an average smaller dog. Labs also need plenty of fresh water and a well-balanced diet.

THINGS THEY NEED

Dogs need a quiet place to sleep. A soft dog bed in a quiet corner is the best place for Labs to sleep. A dog bed can be anything from a special basket to a box. Line the inside with an old blanket or cushion. Once a week, clean the lining of the dog bed.

Labs love winter weather. If the dog lives outside, give it a dry, **insulated** dog house. The dog house should be set on some bricks to raise it off the ground. This keeps the floor of the dog house dry in wet weather.

Labs were born to run. A large fenced-in yard is the perfect home for the dog. If that isn't possible, use a long chain on a runner.

In most cities and towns, a dog must be leashed when going for a walk. Dogs also need a license. These can be purchased where driver's licenses are sold.

Labradors are very active dogs and need a lot of space for running and playing.

PUPPIES

Average female dogs can have from one to eight puppies. The dog is **pregnant** for about nine weeks. When she is ready to give birth, she needs a dark place away from noises. If your dog is pregnant, give her a strong box lined with an old blanket. She will have her puppies there.

Dogs are **mammals**. They drink milk from their mother. After about four weeks, puppies will grow teeth. At this time, separate them from their mother and give the puppies soft dog food.

Your puppy will probably grow up to look like its mother and father.

Labrador puppies need plenty of milk. After about four weeks they can eat soft dog food.

GLOSSARY

BREED - A group of animals with the same traits.

CANIDAE (CAN-ih-day) - The name for the dog family.

CARNIVORES (CAR-nih-vors) - Animals that eat meat. This includes dogs, cats, and humans.

COAT -The dog's outer covering (hair).

DISTEMPER - A contagious disease of dogs and certain other animals, caused by a virus.

HEPATITIS (hep-uh-TIE-tis) - An inflammation of the liver caused by a virus.

INSTINCT - A way of acting that is born in an animal, not learned.

INSULATION (in-sue-LAY-shun) - Something that stops heat loss.

MAMMAL - A class of animals, including humans, that have hair and feed their young milk.

NUTRITION (new-TRISH-un) - Food; nourishment.

PEDIGREE - A chart that lists a dog's ancestors.

PREGNANT - With one or more babies growing inside the body.

PREY - An animal hunted for food.

RETRIEVE - To return or bring back.

SPECIES - A group of related plants or animals.

TRAIT - A feature or characteristic.

Index

BIBLIOGRAPHY

American Kennel Club. *The Complete Dog Book.* New York: Macmillan, 1992.

Clutton-Brock, Juliet. *Dog.* New York: Alfred A. Knopf, 1991.

The Complete Book of the Dog. New York: Holt, Rinehart, & Winston, 1985.

Lord, Suzanne. *The Labrador Retriever.* New York: Crestwood House, 1991.

Sylvester, Patricia. *The Reader's Digest Illustrated Book of Dogs.* New York: The Reader's Digest Association, 1984.

Wolters, Richard A. *The Labrador Retriever: The History....the People.* Los Angeles: Petersen Prints, 1981.